THE CAST OF
GIRL
MEETS WORLD

REAL BIOS

By Marie Morreale

Children's Press®
An Imprint of Scholastic Inc.

Photos ©: cover background: Feaspb/Shutterstock, Inc.; front cover: Araya Diaz/Getty Images; back cover: Lilly Lawrence/WireImage/Getty Images; 1 left, 1 center left: Joey Terrill; 1 center right: Tibrina Hobson/Getty Images; 1 right: Harmony Gerber/Getty Images; 2 background: Feaspb/Shutterstock, Inc.; 2 top: Tibrina Hobson/Getty Images; 2 bottom: Imeh Akpanudosen/Getty Images; 3 background: Feaspb/Shutterstock, Inc.; 3 left: Angela Weiss/Getty Images; 3 right: David Livingston/Getty Images; 4-5 background: Michael Simon/Startraks Photo; 4 top: David Livingston/Getty Images; 4 bottom: Jason LaVeris/FilmMagic; 5 inset: Araya Diaz/Getty Images; 7: Michael Simon/Startraks Photo; 8: s_bukley/Shutterstock, Inc.; 9 top: npine/Shutterstock, Inc.; 9 bottom left: Bill Kostroun/AP Images; 9 bottom right: bestv/Shutterstock, Inc.; 11: John Lamparski/WireImage/Getty Images; 12: Jesse Bauer/Startraks Photo; 13 top left: DFree/Shutterstock, Inc.; 13 top right: Bhofack2/Dreamstime; 13 bottom left: John Lamparski/WireImage/Getty Images; 13 bottom right: BrazilPhotos/Shutterstock, Inc.; 15: Araya Diaz/Getty Images; 16: Charley Gallay/Getty Images for The Weinstein Company; 17 top: alptraum/Thinkstock; 17 center left: Steve Granitz/WireImage/Getty Images; 17 center right: Ken Wolter/Shutterstock, Inc.; 17 bottom: Eric Bakke/AP Images; 19: Angela Weiss/Getty Images; 20: Vivien Killilea/WireImage/Getty Images; 21 top left: GlobalP/Thinkstock; 21 top right: rvlsoft/Thinkstock; 21 bottom left: John E. Kelly/Getty Images; 21 bottom right: Nerthuz/Thinkstock; 22: Touchstone Television/Everett Collection; 24: Everett Collection; 25: infusny-244/INFphoto.com/Newscom; 26: Lilly Lawrence/WireImage; 27 top: Touchstone Television/Everett Collection; 27 bottom: Noam Galai/WireImage/Getty Images; 28: Vincent Sandoval/WireImage/Getty Images; 30: Amy Sussman/Invision/AP Images; 32: Michael Simon/Startraks Photo; 33: Michael Simon/Starktraks Photo; 34: Araya Diaz/Getty Images; 35: David Livingston/Getty Images; 36: Joey Terrill; 37 top: Jason LaVeris/FilmMagic/Getty Images; 37 center: David Livingston/Getty Images; 37 bottom: Imeh Akpanudosen/Getty Images; 38 top left top: Bhofack2/Dreamstime; 38 top left bottom: Jason LaVeris/FilmMagic/Getty Images; 38 top right top: Bochkarev Photography/Shutterstock, Inc.; 38 top right bottom: Imeh Akpanudosen/Getty Images; 38 bottom left top: Sparkia/Dreamstime; 38 bottom left bottom: Vivien Killilea/WireImage/Getty Images; 38 bottom right left: Vorobyeva/Shutterstock, Inc.; 38 bottom right right: Tibrina Hobson/Getty Images; 39: Sara Jaye Weiss/Startraks Photo; 40 top: Araya Diaz/Getty Images; 40 bottom: f11photo/Shutterstock, Inc.; 41 top: Andrey Bayda/Shutterstock, Inc.; 41 center: AndreyPopov/Thinkstock; 41 bottom: RTimages/Shutterstock, Inc.; 42: Lilly Lawrence/WireImage/Getty Images; 43: Weinstein Company/Everett Collection; 44: Chelsea Lauren/Getty Images for The Pantages Theatre.

Library of Congress Cataloging-in-Publication Data
Morreale, Marie.
    The cast of Girl meets world / by Marie Morreale.
        pages cm. — (Real bios)
    Includes bibliographical references and index.
    ISBN 978-0-531-21572-2 (library binding : alk. paper) —
ISBN 978-0-531-21664-4 (pbk. : alk. paper)
1. Girl meets world (Television program)—Juvenile literature.
[1. Actors and actresses—United States—Biography—Juvenile
literature.] I. Title.
    PN1992.77.G55325M67 2016
    791.4502'80922—dc23 [B]   2014049202

© 2016 Scholastic Inc.

All rights reserved. Published in 2015 by Children's Press, an imprint of Scholastic Inc.
Printed in the United States 113

SCHOLASTIC, CHILDREN'S PRESS, and associated logos are trademarks and/or registered trademarks of Scholastic Inc.

1 2 3 4 5 6 7 8 9 10 R 25 24 23 22 21 20 19 18 17 16

Everyone loves the cast of *Girl Meets World*!

MEET THE CAST OF
GIRL MEETS WORLD

The Disney Channel sitcom *Girl Meets World* is heartfelt
and fun, and it has introduced audiences everywhere
to amazing new talent. **Rowan Blanchard . . . Sabrina
Carpenter . . . Peyton Meyer . . . August Maturo**—these
actors have become weekly visitors in millions of homes.
They bring the show's quirky, curious characters to life as
they deal with today's issues and everyday kid experiences.

In this *Real Bio*, you'll get to know Rowan, Sabrina,
Peyton, and August even better! They'll be answering
questions fans have asked, revealing their faves, and
confessing to their most embarrassing moments. If you're
a *GMW* fan, this is a must-read!

CONTENTS

THE CAST OF GIRL MEETS WORLD

The *GMW* cast is thrilled by their fans' loyalty.

SAYVILLE LIBRARY

THE FAB FOUR

ROWAN

THE "IT" GIRL

Rowan Blanchard knew from an early age that she wanted to be an actor. Her parents, Elizabeth and Mark Blanchard-Boulbol, encouraged their talented little girl. But acting was not a Blanchard-Boulbol family tradition. Elizabeth and Mark are yoga instructors!

"I know that everyone says this, but I really have been performing since I was like three," Rowan told Scholastic Classroom Magazines. "I used to put on my own little shows when I was little. Actually, I started professionally acting when I was five, but I think I really connected to acting when I was like seven or eight."

When Rowan was seven, she played a dancing robot in the Disney Junior series *Dance-a-Lot Robot*. Rowan's love of dancing really sparkled on-screen. "The robot is trying to get everyone to dance, because the whole idea of the show is that kids

"ACTING IS FUN . . . YOU GET TO LIVE SOMEONE ELSE'S LIFE!"

To prepare for her role as Riley, Rowan watched every episode of *Boy Meets World*.

Sweet Amanda's

Giggles
"OMG moments happen to me every five minutes."

just are watching TV and they don't really do much," she explained to hollywoodchicago.com.

Rowan was eight years old when she landed her

Rowan was thrilled when she heard she won the role of Riley!

first film role in the movie *The Back-up Plan*. Being on a movie set was exciting, and it was especially thrilling for Rowan because she was reunited with an old friend—Jennifer Lopez! "My dad taught yoga to her," she told hollywoodchicago.com.

The year 2011 was a big one for Rowan. She landed her biggest break—the role of Rebecca in *Spy Kids: All the Time in the World in 4D*. "I never expected to get such a big role," Rowan told *The Star Scoop*. "I **auditioned** for this, not knowing what I was really getting into."

Rowan got an acting education while filming *Spy Kids*. "I learned that it takes more than just actors to make a movie," she continued. "What I mean by that is the [food] service people, the makeup/hair team, special effects, extras and stand-ins . . . it's important to respect those people as well because without them there is no movie."

That attitude made Rowan a true professional by the time she joined *Girl Meets World*.

FACT FILE

NAME: Rowan Eleanor Blanchard

NICKNAME: Row

BIRTHDAY: October 14, 2001

PETS: A golden retriever named Winston

LITTLE-KNOWN TALENTS: Nail polish art and hair braiding

UNUSUAL TALENT: She's a hula-hoop champ

NOT-SO-SECRET SECRET: She's a Broadway trivia expert

FAVORITE SPORTS TEAM: New York Knicks

FAVORITE ATHLETE: NBA star Carmelo Anthony

FAVORITE SINGERS: Adele, Christina Perri, Barbra Streisand, Mumford and Sons

FAVORITE BOOKS: The Outsiders, The Giver, So B. It

FAVORITE BOOK & MOVIE SERIES: The Hunger Games

FAVORITE TV SERIES: Gossip Girls

FAVORITE ACTRESSES: Elle Fanning and Emma Watson

FAVORITE HOBBIES: Cooking—she loves to create her own recipes

FAVORITE CANDY: Hershey's chocolate bars

FAVORITE SNACK: Frozen yogurt, especially from Menchie's

GMW Pals
"It's very surreal! Everyone is so nice!"

THE FAB FOUR
SABRINA

SHE SHINES!

A native of Lehigh Valley, Pennsylvania, Sabrina Carpenter was just a toddler when she first started performing. "I started dance when I was two years old," she told Scholastic Classroom Magazines. "I went to Dance Works in Quakertown, PA. They just had the best teachers." Soon her room was filled with trophies from dancing competitions. When Sabrina was seven, she surprised her parents with a second talent—singing. Off she went to a vocal coach. By the time she was nine, she entered a national singing contest hosted by pop superstar Miley Cyrus. Out of 10,000 entries, Sabrina placed third in the competition. Afterward, a local television reporter interviewed her. When she was asked what her dreams were, Sabrina didn't have to stop and think. "I hope someday to have my own show, and that

BFFs
"True friends will support you no matter what."

Sabrina wowed the *Fox & Friends* audience at the show's 2014 All-American Summer Concert Series.

"I'D LOVE TO SING WITH ADELE ONE DAY!"

little girls will be playing my music at their parties and sleepovers," she said.

Sabrina had proven she was a singer and dancer. The next step was to add acting to the list. Sabrina told Scholastic that she remembered the exact moment when she realized she wanted to use all her talents. "It was actually, believe it or not, when I was watching the very first episode of *Hannah Montana*—it was in 2006," she recalled. "I just remember watching Miley and she was acting and singing and she played this superstar. . . . So I just kind of realized that I really, really wanted to start acting."

By 2010, Sabrina had landed some small film and television roles. She booked roles on Fox's *The Goodwin Games*, the Disney Channel **pilot** *Gulliver Quinn*, the TV movie *The Unprofessional*, and the feature film *Noobz*.

Sabrina walks her dog, Goodwin. They are best buds!

Those roles, combined with commercial jobs, led to the role of Maya on *GMW*. Next was a Hollywood Records recording contract, the release of her first **EP**, *Can't Blame a Girl for Trying*, and her 2015 debut album, *Eyes Wide Open*.

Sabrina was ready for the world to fall in love with her!

FACT FILE

NAME: Sabrina Ann Lynn Carpenter

BIRTHDAY: May 11, 1999

FAVORITE TYPE OF FOOD: Mexican—homemade fajitas

EARLY MUSICAL INFLUENCES: Christina Aguilera, Adele

SIBLINGS: Three sisters (her sister Sarah occasionally appears on GMW)

PETS: A Maltese/ Chihuahua/Yorkie mix named Goodwin and three cats named Woody, Beau, and Junior

HIDDEN TALENT: Drawing

INSTRUMENTS: Guitar and piano

FAVORITE CELEB CRUSH: Ansel Elgort

FAVORITE SOCIAL MEDIA: Instagram

FAVORITE TV SHOW: Pretty Little Liars

FAVORITE DISNEY SERIES: Lizzie McGuire and Wizards of Waverly Place

FAVORITE ACTRESS: Jennifer Lawrence

DREAM PLACE TO VISIT: Paris, France

THE FAB FOUR
PEYTON

HE HITS A HOME RUN!!

On November 24, 1998, Elizabeth and Robert Meyer welcomed their third son, Peyton, into the world. Older brothers Dillon and Cole had hoped for a baby sister, but Peyton quickly became everything the whole family could have wished for. When he started walking, he really started running! When he started talking, he didn't stop.

Peyton was a good student in school, but as a natural athlete, his first love was sports. Baseball was his dream activity. Almost any afternoon, you could find Peyton hitting balls with his buddies.

At the same time, something else caught Peyton's attention—television. He spent tons of time watching his favorite shows and memorizing the characters' lines. When he was 10 years old, he told his parents that he was interested in acting. Elizabeth and Robert weren't so sure.

Green Man
"It's cool to care about the environment."

"LUCAS IS NOT QUITE WHO YOU THINK!"

Peyton is a true-blue Disney kid, with both *Dog with a Blog* and *Girl Meets World* on his resume!

On his 12th birthday, Peyton sat down with them and asked if they would help him make his dream come true. Peyton's parents realized he was very serious. Elizabeth did some investigating and suggested that

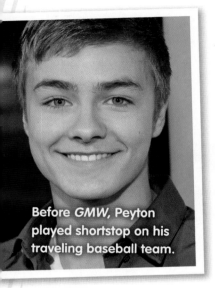

Before *GMW*, Peyton played shortstop on his traveling baseball team.

he enter some local acting contests. At one Las Vegas competition, he did a performance for an audience of talent scouts, **agents**, and managers. Shortly after that, Peyton signed with a talent agency, and his life changed completely.

Peyton's first jobs were commercials and movie trailers. Eventually, the Disney Channel picked him for a guest role on *Dog with a Blog*. The show's creators cast him in several more episodes. Michael Jacobs, the creator of the 1990s hit *Boy Meets World* noticed him while he was prepping the *BMW* spin-off, *Girl Meets World*.

After five auditions, Peyton was cast as Lucas Friar, the romantic interest for Rowan Blanchard's Riley Matthews. "I am the new kid in school and I moved from Austin, Texas, to New York City," Peyton told Scholastic. "So I'm a little bit out of my comfort zone."

Well, now Peyton has found his comfort zone on *GMW*, and he's loving every minute!

FACT FILE

NAME: Peyton Meyer

BIRTHDAY: November 24, 1998

BIRTHPLACE: Las Vegas, Nevada

SIBLINGS: Older brothers Dillon and Cole

PET: A miniature poodle named London

FIRST DREAM: Baseball

SELF-DESCRIPTION: Sarcastic

FIRST FEATURE FILM: Gibby

FUN FACT: Peyton shares a b-day with Modern Family star Sarah Hyland

FAVORITE SINGERS: Justin Bieber, Austin Mahone, One Direction, Sabrina Carpenter, Zendaya, Bella Thorne

FAVORITE SPORTS: Baseball, surfing, and snowboarding

FAVORITE GROUP GAME: Laser tag

FAVORITE CHILDHOOD BOOKS: Lemony Snicket's A Series of Unfortunate Events

FAVORITE FAST-FOOD RESTAURANT: In-N-Out Burger

FAVORITE PASTIME: Hanging with the GMW cast

PEYTON WAS NAMED AFTER NFL SUPERSTAR PEYTON MANNING!

THE FAB FOUR
AUGGIE

MEANT FOR THE STAGE!

A true-blue California boy, August Maturo was born in the beautiful city of Ventura. Nestled on the Pacific coast, it is the perfect spot for a young family with showbiz hopes. It's just far enough away from the cray-cray of Hollywood, yet close enough to get there by car.

When he was four, August appeared in a church play. Right then and there, he knew where he belonged—in Hollywood! He began urging his parents to make the drive to the center of superstar dreams.

"In my heart I always wanted to be on a stage," August told *Celebrity News*. "So my mom found me an agent." The agent had little difficulty finding work for the charming, curly-haired cutie. August started out filming commercials. It was fun, but he was eager for more! He wanted to see scripts. Believe it or not, he could

Mom & Pop

Cory and Topanga are August's fave GMW characters!

AUGUST LOVES TO MAKE PEOPLE LAUGH!

When asked for his advice to kids who want to act, Auggie said, "It takes lots of practice, and never ever give up!"

August is an animal lover, and dogs are his favorite!

even decide if a certain role was right for him. He had learned to read when he was just two years old!

August's first major acting gig was the role of Isaac in the TV movie *Applebaum*. He quickly followed that up with a recurring role in *How I Met Your Mother* and guest spots on the shows *Dads*, *See Dad Run*, *Raising Hope*, and *Suburgatory*. That was a pretty impressive resume for a boy who hadn't reached his seventh birthday! But it got even better. August was eventually cast as Auggie Matthews, Riley's little brother on *Girl Meets World*.

As soon as the *GMW* contracts were signed, the six-year-old started doing his acting homework. "After I was cast," August told *Celebrity News*, "I watched all of *Boy Meets World* Season 1 because they are appropriate for my age!"

It was a good study. He really learned about the characters, especially Cory and Topanga, who would be his parents on *GMW*. "Auggie's kind of funny, interesting," he told Scholastic. "He wants to be like his dad, Cory."

AUGUST WANTS TO GET A DOG AND NAME IT KOROKAS— "IT'S LIKE A MAGIC PUPPY!"

FACT FILE

NAME: August Maturo

BIRTHDAY: August 28, 2007

BIRTHPLACE: Ventura, California

SIBLING: Younger brother, Ocean

CURRENT PET: A fish

DREAM PET: Dalmatian puppy

DREAM CAREER: Singer

FUN FACT: August shares a b-day with actor Jack Black

FAVORITE BREAKFAST: Pancakes and eggs

FAVORITE FAST-FOOD RESTAURANT: Denny's

FAVORITE CANDY: Chocolate

FAVORITE PART OF ACTING: Red carpet appearances and interviews

FAVORITE SPORT: Rock climbing

FAVORITE MOVIES: Home Alone and Home Alone 2

FAVORITE MOVIE DIRECTOR: Chris Columbus

FAVORITE CHILDHOOD BOOK: Goldilocks and the Three Bears

FAVORITE INSTRUMENT: Piano

FAVORITE SCHOOL SUBJECTS: Geography and math

The original cast of
Boy Meets World

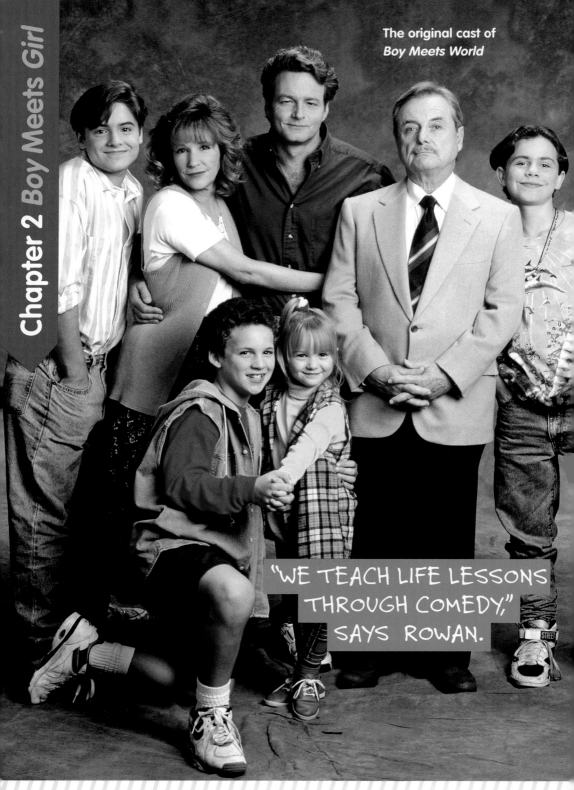

"WE TEACH LIFE LESSONS
THROUGH COMEDY,"
SAYS ROWAN.

BOY MEETS GIRL!

REBOOT, TELEVISION STYLE

Back in the 1990s, the sitcom *Boy Meets World* had kids all across the country glued to their TVs. Viewers could laugh and relate to the situations the characters experienced. Ben "Cory" Savage, Danielle "Topanga" Fishel, Rider "Shawn" Strong, Will "Eric" Friedle, and the long list of other costars became BFFs to the show's fans.

When the last episode of *BMW* aired on May 5, 2000, the producers, cast, and crew had mixed feelings. They were happy about moving on to new projects, but they were sad that their second home was being boarded up.

After *BMW* ended, whole new generations became fans through **syndication** on TV. The reruns were so successful, there was chatter about creating a *BMW* spinoff. The Disney Channel reached out to *BMW*'s original

Real vs Reel
Just like Riley, Rowan's dad is one of her teachers!

Rider Strong (left) and Ben Savage (right) were just teens in *Boy Meets World*.

co-creator, Michael Jacobs, but he wasn't crazy about the idea at first. "I got a phone call, 'We love *Boy Meets World*. Could we do this again in some capacity?'" he told *Entertainment Weekly*. "And my answer was no."

The Disney execs were surprised, but Ben Savage later explained to TVGuide.com, "I think there was a little bit of hesitation because we just wanted to make sure that if we were gonna come back . . . we wanted to do something that we're all proud of."

GMW's Timeline

As the World Turns

JUNE 17, 2013
Disney approves the *Girl Meets World* project

APRIL 10, 2014
Disney Channel releases the first teaser for *GMW*

APRIL 26, 2014
The full *GMW* cast is introduced at the 2014 Radio Disney Music Awards

MAY 2, 2014
A full *GMW* trailer is released

WHY DOES AUGUST LIKE AUGGIE? "HE'S ME!" HE LAUGHS.

Jacobs didn't want a new show just to be a sequel of *BMW*. He wanted it to be "real life"—meaning that the plot would be centered on a married Cory and Topanga raising their two kids, Riley and Auggie. Jacobs would not commit until he made sure the former stars wanted to return to their roles. At first, they weren't crazy about the idea either. But after knocking around some ideas with Jacobs, Ben changed his mind. Things were on a roll.

As the show developed, its creators decided to focus on Cory and Topanga's tween daughter, Riley—thus the title, *Girl Meets World*. It would deal with today's situations in a very modern way. "It's just a much different place now than it was in 1993 when I met the world," Ben told TVGuide.com. "It's a much more interesting and complicated time to be a kid."

MAY 19, 2014
GMW's theme song, "Take on the World," is released, sung by Sabrina and Rowan

JUNE 27, 2014
GMW premieres on the Disney Channel

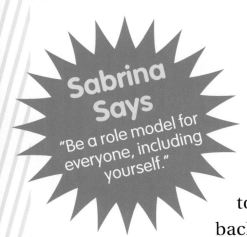

The audition process started. Rowan tried out early on. Though Jacobs really liked her, he felt at first that she was too young for the role of Riley. Luckily the process of planning out the show took over a year, and Rowan came back in for another audition. She had grown up. "As soon as Rowan walked into the room, I was reminded of why Ben Savage was loved as Cory Matthews," Jacobs told insidetv.ew.com.

The new characters of Riley Matthews, Auggie Matthews, Maya Hart, Lucas Friar, and Farkle were soon cast. As word got out that *Girl Meets World* was coming soon, fans were thrilled—and so was the new cast. "I screamed when I got the part," Rowan told *People* magazine. "And I totally geeked out when I met Danielle and Ben. I was like, 'I want to be your daughter!'"

JULY 22, 2014
Sabrina performs at the 2014 WEE ROCK! Kids Music Festival

AUGUST 6, 2014
GMW is renewed for a second season

AUGUST 10, 2014
GMW is nominated for Choice Summer TV Show at the Teen Choice Awards

NOVEMBER 5, 2014
The second season of *GMW* begins shooting

Danielle Fishel and Ben Savage (seen here in a still from *Boy Meets World*) are now everyone's favorite TV parents as Topanga and Cory!

By the time *GMW* started taping, Sabrina told a Scholastic interviewer, "Honestly it's overwhelming in an amazing way. I never experienced anything like this in my life. And I think it's really good that kids are finding it relatable."

Judging by *GMW*'s runaway success, it looks like the world is hearing the message loud and clear!

NOVEMBER 27, 2014
Sabrina appears in the 2014 Macy's Thanksgiving Day Parade

FALL 2015
Rowan stars in the Disney TV movie *Invisible Sister*

FALL 2016
Sabrina stars in the Disney TV movie *Further Adventures in Babysitting*

Sabrina, Rowan, Core and August attend a screening of *Pants on Fire*

IN THE SPOTLIGHT

GET TO KNOW ROWAN, SABRINA, PEYTON, AND AUGUST!

W ant to find out what Rowan likes to read? What Sabrina's middle school days were like? What Peyton thinks about the environment? What August likes to do when he isn't acting? Well, read on and you'll find the answers to all of these questions . . . and lots more!

ROWAN

On watching *Boy Meets World* . . . "It hasn't gone off the air since it started, which is pretty incredible. So reruns play all the time. And I had seen some episodes before, but obviously, when I booked the show, I went back and I watched all of it again."

On her favorite subject, math . . . "It's something that has always come naturally to me. But I love that it's definite answers and I love working with numbers. I find

Sabrina and Rowan are all smiles for the camera.

it fun. And I know that most people hate math, but it's something that I've always found to be my strength."

On her favorite book . . . ""I think my favorite book is *The Outsiders*. You know that [S. E. Hinton] started it when she was 15 and finished it when she was 17. It's so incredible because I think a lot of books tend to shy away from what kids really are doing and how kids really feel, and I feel like because she was that age while she was writing *The Outsiders*, that's what makes it so truthful and honest."

On when she likes to read . . . "When I'm on a plane. And certainly when I go to sleep. But I think I kind of read for inspiration. Like after I read a book I'm like, 'Oh, I want to write now.'"

On what she would do if she could control the world . . . "This is a tough one! I would make [people] give me all the chocolate in the world."

On the three things she would take to a desert island . . . "Oh my goodness. My whole family is one thing, Sabrina, and then my dog, Winston."

On what she does in her spare time . . . "Watch movies . . . To cook, it is strawberry cupcakes, or to bake. To eat, chocolate. Just chocolate."

SABRINA

On writing songs . . . "When I was about 10 years old, I would write stuff in my notebook, but it's nothing that I'd ever want anybody in the world to hear. So I think I really started writing when I was 13, 14. You know, and it's so different now because I'm writing with some great writers and I'm collaborating with people and I'm just learning so much about it that I never knew before."

On the music she listened to when she was in middle school . . . "I listened to so many people. I

listened to Taylor Swift. I can remember listening to 'Our Song' for the first time on the school bus. My friend introduced me to her. I always listened to Christina Aguilera because I was doing lots of [her] numbers in dance school. Obviously Britney, so I listened to a lot of them in middle school."

On getting embarrassed . . . "I was kind of a joker in class, so I remember raising my hand a lot and instead of giving serious answers, I would make a joke and my teachers would get mad at me. But I was always just trying to lighten up the group. I guess I don't really get embarrassed because when I'm around a familiar group of people that I'm so comfortable with, I just laugh everything off. And even if it's embarrassing, you just forget about it and have fun."

Sabrina kicks it up for her "The Middle of Starting Over" video.

Sabrina and her backup dancers for "The Middle of Starting Over"

On her least favorite subject in school . . . "Math . . . only because I've never been great at it. I'm more artsy."

On her personal motto . . . "I live by staying humble and I think that's one of the things I keep to my heart all the time. And also, 'When one door closes, another door opens,' because in this business you definitely have to deal with rejection a lot."

On her favorite book/movie series . . . "Not gonna lie. I'm obsessed with Harry Potter now! I've watched five movies in three days since I've been to the studio tour!"

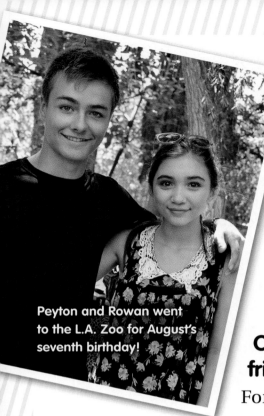
Peyton and Rowan went to the L.A. Zoo for August's seventh birthday!

On *Girl Meets World's* plot lines compared to *Boy Meets World* . . .

"Most of the same things, but I mean now all the *Boy Meets World* fans get to see Ben and Danielle as adults now instead of kids."

On if Lucas would be his friend in real life . . . "Oh yes. For sure."

On what Danielle Fishel and Ben Savage have taught the kids on set . . . "Every day they tell us stuff that will help our acting or help our role."

On how kids should help the environment . . .

"You know, I mean, every kid has to go to school and every kid there is going to have a lot of kids with them. So I would tell them to tell all their friends and all the other kids that it's cool to care about the environment."

On his life motto . . . "Never let the fear of striking out get in your way!"

AUGUST

On playing a character with his own name . . .
"Fun." [Laughs]

On what he likes to do when he's not in school or acting . . . "I like to hang out with my cast mates or go up to their rooms. I always want to go to Peyton's room to play with London—London is his dog. They named it London because they had another dog, but it died and it was named Paris."

On his favorite thing about going to New York City for a GMW appearance . . . "My favorite thing I've done so far is doing like photos, interviews, like red carpets. . . . And we woke up early, we went to Central Park and rock climbed. And my little brother made it up a big rock!"

August loves to go to movies and the theater. Acting is his thing!

On why he likes playing Auggie . . . "My favorite part is that he is funny and I love to make people laugh!"

FACETIME WITH *GMW* CAST

GIGGLE-WORTHY FACTS & TRIVIA

ROWAN ON RILEY

"Riley Matthews is the daughter of Cory and Topanga. She is 12 years old and in seventh grade. She's extremely silly and quirky, but I think what makes Riley so special is that she's so extremely loyal to everyone."

Rowan thinks that Riley on *GMW* is the ultimate role!

SABRINA ON MAYA

"[Maya] is the troublemaker of life. The cool thing about her is she [has] this guard around her. She has got this force field around her and I think that is why she has this tough, sarcastic humor. She kind of uses that to hide . . . her family life."

AUGUST ON AUGGIE

"I'm different [from Auggie] because I am not so girl crazy! I am like Auggie because I'm smart and I'm a good boy."

PEYTON ON LUCAS

"I love my character because, you know, he always knows the right thing to do and stays [true] to what he believes is right."

FOODIE FUN

SABRINA

IF SHE COULD MAKE HER OWN FLAVOR OF ICE CREAM . . .

"I'm obsessed with mint, so I think anything mint flavored and maybe some cookie dough and dark chocolate, then maybe some … is it weird if I add lemon? I'd call it 'Sabtastic'!"

PEYTON

THANKSGIVING FAMILY TRADITION . . .

The whole family gathers the day after Turkey Day to watch Peyton and brother Dillon pull the turkey wishbone! But the boys can't reveal their wishes!

AUGUST

FAVORITE MEAL TO EAT OUT . . .

"I'm a vegetarian kind of. My little brother eats the meat. When we go to Denny's we just ask for pancakes and eggs, no sausage. And chocolate. Chocolate chip pancakes."

ROWAN

FAVORITE FOODS . . .

"Pasta and sushi! I love, love, love sushi!"

FASHIONISTAS
Rowan and Sabrina share their style secrets

ROWAN

"Getting to express yourself through fashion is fantastic. It's fun to take fashion risks. . . . You'll never know until you try!"

"SABRINA AND I FACETIME EACH OTHER DURING THE RIDE HOME FROM THE SET."—ROWAN

SABRINA

"Fashion is a great way to express yourself, and wearing an outfit you love gives you confidence."

Rowan and Sabrina became besties on the set of *GMW*.

QUICKIE ON COREY

NAME: Corey Fogelmanis

BIRTHDAY: August 13, 1999

BIRTH SIGN: Leo

BIRTHPLACE: Los Angeles, California

SELF-DESCRIPTION: Down-to-earth

UNUSUAL TALENT: Tap dancing

FUN FACT: Shamus Farkle was the original name of Corey's character; it was changed to Farkle Minkus

FAVORITE HOBBIES: Dancing and gymnastics

FAVORITE DISNEY CHANNEL STAR: Demi Lovato

FAVORITE BOOK SERIES: Harry Potter

FIRST FILM ROLE: *The Maiden and the Princess* (2011)

EITHER/OR QUIZ

It's up to you to guess the selections of the *GMW* cast! (Answers below)

Broadway . . . is this where you would find Rowan during an NYC visit?

ROWAN
1. **Books: hardcover** or **e-book?**
2. **Entertainment: Broadway musical** or **movie musical?**

SABRINA
3. **Harry Potter** or **American Girl?**
4. **Math** or **English?**

PEYTON
5. ***Dog with a Blog*** or ***Wizards of Waverly Place?***
6. **Basketball** or **baseball?**

AUGUST
7. **Sausages** or **salads?**
8. **Interviews** or **photo shoots?**

COREY
9. **Harry Potter** or **Draco Malfoy?**
10. **Environmentalist** or **litterbug?**

EITHER/OR ANSWERS
1. Hardcover, 2. Broadway, 3. Harry Potter, 4. English, 5. Dog with a Blog, 6. Baseball, 7. Salads, 8. Interviews, 9. Harry Potter, 10. Environmentalist

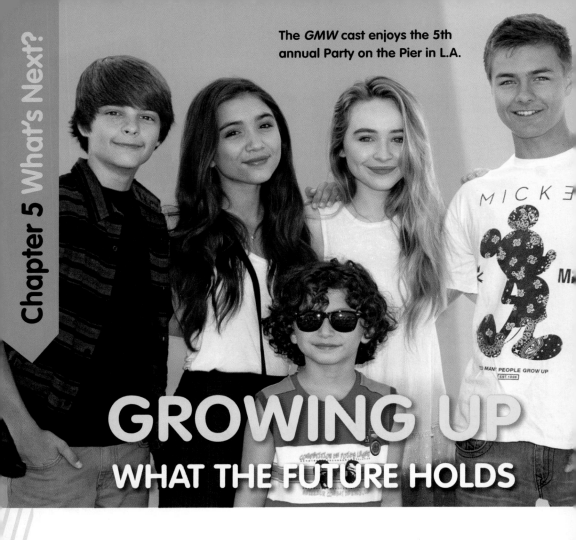

The *GMW* cast enjoys the 5th annual Party on the Pier in L.A.

GROWING UP
WHAT THE FUTURE HOLDS

Even though *Girl Meets World* is still fairly new, fans want to know what's going to happen next to both the characters and the cast. What happens to the characters is all up to producer/creator Michael Jacobs and the *GMW* writers. As for the cast, that's a different story. As working actors, they all hope to continue entertaining audiences everywhere. But there are a few curves in the road ahead of them.

According to producer Michael Jacobs, Rowan has a long career ahead of her. Even though he once passed on her

because she was too young, her second audition proved that she was a natural-born actress. When Jacobs had her read lines for Disney's top executives, they were blown away. "It was our first breath of real honesty, that this was a real girl who was actually growing up," Jacobs told *The Hollywood Reporter*. "We came to love her quirkiness and naturalness. Rowan instructed us that this is the show we should be doing."

She proved him right. Before *GMW*, Rowan had appeared in one feature film, *Spy Kids: All the Time in the World in 4D*. In 2015, she signed on for the film *A World Away* and the Disney TV movie *Invisible Sister*. There is also some talk about a singing career—after all, she and Sabrina did sing *GMW*'s theme song, "Take on the World." "My music will be a mix of everything!" Rowan told *The Star Scoop*. "Not just pop, but something for everyone."

Rowan plans on having a long, long career!

Of course, there is one particular dream Rowan hopes will come true—being in a Broadway musical! "It's one of my main goals in life," she told thecelebritycafe.com. "I really want to get there. I love to do acting, singing, and dancing so it would be awesome to be on there."

Then there is Sabrina. When she signed on to play Maya, she had to learn to juggle two careers. She had already established herself as an actress. She had either costarred or guest-starred in nearly a dozen TV series. She also signed on for the 2016 Disney TV movie *Further Adventures in Babysitting*.

"THE FIRST SEASON HAS BEEN ONE BIG LEARNING EXPERIENCE." —SABRINA

But Sabrina's other goal was to release an album. In April 2014, she released a four-song EP, *Can't Blame a Girl for Trying*. It did so well that Hollywood Records scheduled a full-length album for 2015. While Sabrina was working on *GMW*, she was also writing songs and going into the studio to record whenever she could. Sabrina has set goals for both her acting and singing careers, and she's well on her way.

Peyton has always loved acting and was thrilled when he first joined the Disney Channel family with his role on *Dog with a Blog*. When he was picked to play Lucas on *GMW*, he knew he was setting solid ground for a long-term acting career. This was proven true when he landed a role in the 2015 movie *Gibby*. Peyton loved every minute on the *Gibby* set, especially when he had to work with Crystal, the capuchin monkey who plays the title character!

And then there's August. If anyone is headed for stardom, it's this energetic young actor. By the time he was seven years old, he was already an experienced pro. His mom has said he knew he wanted to be an actor the minute he was born! When *Celebrity News* asked August about his roles so far, he enthused, "I remember all of them, and they were all great! But my first role was the [TV movie] *Applebaum* directed by Christopher Columbus, who directed *Home Alone 1* and *2*, and those are my favorite movies! That was so exciting!"

August has said that he has learned a lot from Chris Columbus and Michael Jacobs. He always wants to learn new things. So don't be surprised if August adds the titles of "director" and "producer" to his resume!

Rowan, Sabrina, Peyton, and August all have a bright future ahead. They can't wait to find out where their talent and drive will take them!

Surprise!
Rowan first auditioned for the role of Maya on *GMW*.

Resources

BLOG
Morreale, Marie, *Girl Meets World Interviews*, New York: Scholastic Web site: THE STACKS/INK SPLOT, 2014.

ARTICLES
Gonzalez, Sandra. "On 'Girl Meets World,' Ben Savage and Danielle Fishel Meet Parenting." New York: *Entertainment Weekly*, 2014.

Dodds, Eric. "Girl Meets World: An Interview With Star Ben Savage," New York: *Time*, 2014.

Facts for Now

Visit this Scholastic Web site for more information on **The Cast of Girl Meets World**:
www.factsfornow.scholastic.com
Enter the keywords **Girl Meets World**

Glossary

agents *(AY-juhnts)* people who work with actors, singers, and other entertainers to help them find work

auditioned *(aw-DISH-uhnd)* gave a short performance to compete for a part in a play, film, or television show

EP *(EE PEE)* short for "extended play"; an EP is shorter than a full album but longer than a single

pilot *(PYE-luht)* a single episode of a TV show that is used to determine whether an entire series should be produced

syndication *(sin-duh-KAY-shuhn)* the process of airing reruns of a TV show on a number of different channels

Index

Acknowledgments

Page 6: Performing: Scholastic Classroom Magazines October 2013; Acting: Scholastic Classroom Magazines October 2013; *Dance-a-Lot-Robot*: hollywoodchicago.com August 16, 2011
Page 7: Giggles: *Bop* September 2014
Page 8: Jennifer Lopez: hollywoodchicago.com August 16, 2011; *Spy Kids 4D: The Star Scoop* September 26, 2011
Page 9: *GMW* Pals: Radio Disney
Page 10: Dance Works: Scholastic Classroom Magazines October 17, 2013; Own show: RockyCoastnews.com February 17, 2012; BFFs: *J-14* September 2014
Page 11: Adele: *Tiger Beat* December 2014
Page 12: Miley Cyrus contest: Scholastic Classroom Magazines October 17, 2013
Page 14: Green Man: Scholastic Classroom Magazines June 23, 2014
Page 15: Lucas: Scholastic Classroom Magazines June 23, 2014
Page 16: Lucas/new kid: Twitter November 1, 2014
Page 18: On stage: *Celebrity News* August 18, 2014

Page 20: *BMW* Season 1: *Celebrity News* August 18, 2014; Auggie: Scholastic Classroom Magazines June 23, 2014; Magic puppy: Scholastic Classroom Magazines June 23, 2014
Page 22: Life lessons: Scholastic Classroom Magazines June 23, 2014
Page 23: *BMW* Spinoff: *Entertainment Weekly* February 15, 2013
Page 24: Hesitation: TVGuide.com June 26, 2014
Page 25: Ben agrees: TVGuide.com June 26, 2014
Page 26: Michael Jacobs on Rowan: insidetv.ew.com January 28, 2013; Got the part: *People* July 7, 2014
Page 27: Kids relatable: Scholastic Classroom Magazines June 23, 2014
Page 29: *Boy Meets World*: Scholastic Classroom Magazines June 23, 2014
Page 29: Math: Scholastic Classroom Magazines June 23, 2014
Page 30: Favorite book: Scholastic Classroom Magazines June 23, 2014
Page 30: Read: Scholastic Classroom Magazines June 23, 2014
Page 31: Control the world: Scholastic Classroom Magazines June 23, 2014; Desert island: Scholastic

Classroom Magazines June 23, 2014; Spare time: Scholastic Classroom Magazines June 23, 2014; Writing songs: Scholastic Classroom Magazines June 23, 2014; Middle school music: Scholastic Classroom Magazines June 23, 2014
Page 32: Embarrassed: Scholastic Classroom Magazines June 23, 2014
Page 33: Math: Scholastic Classroom Magazines June 23, 2014; Personal motto: Scholastic Classroom Magazines June 23, 2014; Favorite book/movie series: *Popstar!* September 2014
Page 34: *GMW* plot lines: Scholastic Classroom Magazines June 23, 2014; Lucas: Scholastic Classroom Magazines June 23, 2014; Ben & Danielle: Scholastic Classroom Magazines June 23, 2014; Environment: Scholastic Classroom Magazines June 23, 2014; Life motto: Instagram
Page 35: Character's name: Scholastic Classroom Magazines June 23, 2014; Hanging out: Scholastic Classroom Magazines June 23, 2014; New York City: Scholastic Classroom Magazines June 23, 2014; Playing Auggie: thetvaddict.com August 15, 2014

Page 36: Rowan on Riley: Scholastic Classroom Magazines June 23, 2014
Page 37: Sabrina on Maya: themagazine.ca September 12, 2014; August on Auggie: *Celebrity News* August 18, 2014; Peyton on Lucas: Scholastic Classroom Magazines June 23, 2014
Page 38: Ice cream: Scholastic Classroom Magazines June 23, 2014; Favorite meal: Scholastic Classroom Magazines June 23, 2014; Favorite foods: Scholastic Classroom Magazines June 23, 2014
Page 39: Rowan on fashion: *GL* June/July 2014; Sabrina on fashion: *Twist* September 2014; FaceTime: *Entertainment Weekly* June 13, 2014
Page 43: Michael Jacobs on Rowan: *Hollywood Reporter* January 30, 2013; Rowan on music: *Star Scoop* September 26, 2011; Rowan on Riley: *Entertainment Weekly* February 15, 2013
Page 44: Rowan/Broadway: thecelebritycafe.com July 29, 2011; First season: themagazine.ca
Page 45: *Applebaum*: *Celebrity News* August 8, 2014

About the Author

Marie Morreale is the author of many official and unofficial celebrity biographies. She attended New York University as an English/creative writing major and began her writing and editorial career in New York City. As the editor of teen/music magazines *Teen Machine* and *Jam!*, she covered TV, film, and music personalities and interviewed superstars such as Michael Jackson, Britney Spears, and Justin Timberlake/*NSYNC. Morreale was also an editor/writer at Little Golden Books.

Today, she is the executive editor, Media, of Scholastic Classroom Magazines writing about pop-culture, sports, news, and special events. Morreale lives in New York City and is entertained daily by her two Maine coon cats, Cher and Sullivan.